Seeing

Justice

JANICE NOLAND

WESTBOW
PRESS
A DIVISION OF THOMAS NELSON

WestBow Press books may be ordered through booksellers or by contacting:

WestBow Press
A Division of Thomas Nelson
1663 Liberty Drive
Bloomington, IN 47403
www.westbowpress.com
1-(866) 928-1240

Scripture taken from the King James Version of the Bible.

ISBN: 978-1-4497-9724-9 (sc)
ISBN: 978-1-4497-9725-6 (hc)
ISBN: 978-1-4497-9723-2 (e)

Library of Congress Control Number: 2013910069

Printed in the United States of America.

WestBow Press rev. date: 8/26/2013

DEDICATION

I dedicate this book to my entire family:

My mother and father who taught me as a young
child to accept Jesus Christ as my Lord and Savior; My
husband who read the Word of God to me nightly; and
My three daughters who are carrying this faith forward
into our grandchildren and great-grandchildren.

TABLE OF CONTENTS

INTRODUCTION

This book is intended to acknowledge and glorify the Lord Jesus Christ. It chronicles the life of an American woman who enters the legal profession at a time when women rarely, if ever, chose to pursue that path. That woman was me. My story unfolds with the Lord Jesus Christ becoming the director of my path from its inception, to the present date, and throughout my eternity.

By following His direction, He prepared me for the journey through various experiences. These experiences illumined my path and served to emphasize what would become my passion...the pursuit of justice. I always wanted justice. The real question was just how often and how easily justice could be found?

I began to see a pattern in the courtroom. Seeing justice depended on the Lord's presence, not a blindfolded young woman. I found this to be true irrespective of which client I chose to represent, how effectively the other side presented its case, and even despite the judicial decision maker's demeanor and intent.

And I saw more. I saw injustice play most emphatically in certain areas such as politics and in the news media where falsehood seemed to dominate. I hated injustice where I saw it, but I knew it did not have to prevail. I had witnessed too much good within this country for it to be otherwise.

As I pursued justice I learned some very clear yet simple principles. I learned what it was that the Lord was requiring of us, His followers. He tells us over and over in His Word and He establishes an unequivocal standard by which we are to govern our behavior.

First, we must find God through His Son, our Lord and Savior Jesus Christ. Then we must simply:

Hate evil – Psalm 97:10; and

Hold fast to what is good – 1 Thessalonians 5:21.

I pray you enjoy this journey with me as we pursue justice together.

See Justice

The following pages are unique glimpses of this amazing journey I would undergo with the Lord and how He tangibly made His presence known to me.

Chapter One

Growing Up in St. Louis, Missouri

*In all thy ways acknowledge Him and He
shall direct thy paths.* Prov. 3:6

A life cannot be truly assessed outside the context of its past. My heritage resides in the city where I was born and raised, St. Louis, Missouri. I am a fourth generation American citizen. (Both my parents were one hundred percent German.) I am lucky enough to have a copy of my father's grandfather's citizenship papers which were issued by the Court of Criminal Correction in St. Louis County, September 16, 1868. This great-great grandfather renounced the King of Prussia and became a citizen here. My paternal grandfather continued his father's pursuit of the American Dream. He built a four family flat, as it was called, in St. Louis, which would eventually be my childhood home. My mother's father also built his life in St. Louis, working as a horticulturist in a city park in the southern part of the city. Though my family experienced the joys and freedoms that came with being an American, they also tasted the hardships.

My maternal grandfather lost his job the day after the election in 1932 during the time my father described as "when the banks were closed and the bottles opened." Even as a dentist, if my father received a paltry two dollars cash payment this was appreciated as a payment on account. He lived in a time when few had any money to pay, but my father, a good man, would forgo requiring payments in advance. The times and circumstances of the Depression were undoubtedly hard, but a strong American citizenship sustained.

My grandfather's flat, with white stone steps and all brick, provided the comfortable and secure stage on which my childhood played. The world in which I spent my formative years remains dear to me. I walked five blocks from my home to the public school every day from the first to eighth grade. No one saw the need to provide buses as everyone lived within walking distance.

My memories of my time at elementary school are fond. I remember an iron fence in the schoolyard, which separated the boys and girls at recess. Classes included Christian songs. There was no agenda to block the teaching and knowledge of God. The children were quiet and respectful in class. I recall churning milk in kindergarten and making butter and drinking buttermilk. In kindergarten, the children were all in a band where the instruments were provided by the school. I loved playing the cymbals.

The students were not the only active participants in this academic community. Our parents came to meetings about once a month at school in the evening. These meetings were fun, as we were all like a family coming together. This "family" was not excessively large. In eight grades there were generally 30 children in each class. Yet even among a relatively limited number compared to the number of children in urban schools today, the community spirit was remarkable. Parents and children alike were grateful for the school.

In addition to being a comfortable and happy place, school was also safe. Walking to school, we had guards, eighth grade boys from school, on each corner merely to ensure traffic safety. There was no other concern except good conduct.

Besides home and school, the biggest part of my world was church. From the time my sister and I were three, my parents took us to service each Sunday. In fourteen years, we girls were never allowed to miss worship, unless we were sick.

Like school, the church was about five blocks away. We had no car, so we as a family would always walk. The path to church was comprised of sidewalks and provided a pleasant and safe journey each week.

There are a few other sweet memories from this time in my life. In the evenings, we would sit on the front porch. The lamplighter would walk and light the street lights. There was a man who pushed a cart down the street crying, "hot tamales, get your hot tamales here." Then, on special occasions, we bought a nickel ice cream bar at the corner delicatessen. It is remarkable the resonance the simple pleasures of childhood have on a life.

High School

After elementary school, my world extended. The distance from my home to the high school was measured as a mile as opposed to the few blocks of my elementary school. Despite the greater distance, I walked to school at least for the first two years. The second half I would occasionally choose to ride a bus.

As far as overall experience, my time in high school was much like my time in elementary. The atmospheres of both schools were so much alike. Everyone seemed grateful for the chance to attend a good school with good teachers to get a good education.

Two of my most memorable classes were Latin and swimming. For two years I studied Latin. God was directing my curriculum because at the time I had no idea I would choose the legal profession where such knowledge becomes expedient. Swimming was memorable not because I would later find it necessary for my vocation, but because my kind teacher left such a lasting impression on me. When I took the class, I was fourteen and terrified of getting in the water. I remember breaking out with hives before I had to dive into the pool. But my teacher was so special; she was just determined to help me. Even though she couldn't get in the pool herself, as her legs were bandaged for varicose veins, she used kindness and encouragement to help me overcome my fear.

While everyone may have stories from their education that are personal, that special class or beloved teacher, most also have a memory of some national event which changed their generation. Vietnam, the Cold War, 9/11. For me and my generation, it was World War II.

I was in my second year of high school when December 7, 1941 happened. It spoiled the quiet comfort and safety we had known both as a nation here in the U.S., and also as I experienced it in my world within St. Louis. We truly believed the attacks would continue here. History tells that they never did, but our lives changed nonetheless. I remember air raid sirens and drills where my father, as an air raid warden, would walk the area around our home, all lights out. At the school they held a general assembly where the teachers tried to quiet and calm all the nervous students who were hounded by nightmares of bombers flying over our horizon.

Immediately the nation entered war mode. I have heard the statistic that 400,000 Americans were killed in this war. For me, that's not just a number. It's the number of boys from home that went and laid down their lives. Nearly everyone was called; families torn from each other by the call of duty. Luckily, my home was spared. My father was required to register, but he wasn't called. He said he was too young for the First World War and too old for the second one.

With the war came rationing. Shoes became limited, and we needed coupons to get three pair. It seems like everything was rationed; sugar sticks out, though I don't know why. The rationings seemed to be such a big thing back then, but looking back, nothing seems too extreme. Maybe it was just the change that took such a large place in my young conscious. That once it was one way and now, after this tragedy had happened, it wasn't that way anymore.

Not all changes were bad, though. After a decade of living through the Depression, jobs were good. Rosie the riveter did well. Those who worked in production of war products had plenty of industry for themselves as all of our wonderful service men gave their lives to save our country and our allies. The saying at the time was as later told to me, "To solve the Depression, Roosevelt tried PWA & WPA, and finally WAR."

It was in this world that I completed my last two years in high school. I would go to school in the dark because the government's new implementation of time changes. (Daylight Savings Time continues to this day; I still hate it.) But despite this introduction of a new darkness, both literal and metaphorical, into my world, my time at school was still good. And I could always find the light whenever I looked for it. For instance, once a week, during school hours, I was allowed as a public school student to go to a church of my choice for an hour.

University

After high school, I expanded my horizons once again, starting at Washington University in St. Louis. Though Washington University is undoubtedly a renowned academic institution, I didn't accept the scholarship to attend there for its substantial reputation, but rather because I did not want to leave my home. Also in choosing the university, I had to decide my major.

When I began my college career attending Washington University, my parents tried to assist me in the decisions I was going to have to make in pursuit of knowledge. My father wanted me to pick a profession and follow it through. He encouraged me to shoot for the stars and be a doctor or lawyer even at a time when women lawyers were unheard of. He also said get your degree before you even think about getting married. My mother agreed, but preferred art, where I showed some natural ability. Again they told me to pray for guidance and direction in where and how to make my choices.

I prayed and I chose law as a profession. No great drive or clear direction, but I can say the Lord had a plan for my life; I did not always understand where He was guiding me, but I obediently followed. This book details the adventures of law and how the Lord Jesus Christ was with me every step of the way. His guidance and mercy as I walked through life's tribulations comes to light in the pages you are about to read.

I graduated from law school and passed the bar at the age of twenty-one, at a time when women lawyers constituted approximately two percent of the entire number of those actively practicing law.

During my time at Washington University, I had three major experiences which I wish to share now.

In my first summer at the university I was enrolled in a philosophy class. The professor of the class was a visiting professor. His very first lecture was an adamant defense of evolution. I was only seventeen, but even at that young age I perceived that this professor had his own message and it was destruction of any belief in God. Faced for possibly the first time in my life with a liberal agenda attacking my faith, I found the courage to defend my beliefs.

On every issue, the professor and I were diametrically opposed, and I voiced my contestations. I was the only student in that class who ever stood for a Biblical worldview. The class consisted of teachers getting summer credit. One kindly lady said to me, "You don't even have a philosophy yet." But you know, I did. My parents had helped to instill in me a faith in God and doing good that was apparently stronger in me, a young person, stronger than all the other class members.

I realize that the other students didn't see their silent acceptance as weakness or cowardice. Perhaps they agreed with the professor, though I doubt it, as his convictions were not so widely accepted as today. Most likely they thought they were being smarter than I, choosing to forgo this battle with a professor. Yet what I instinctively felt then and know now is that we need to stand against evil and "hold fast to good." Since that day, the perceptive and authoritative dismissal of my beliefs is something I have fought all my life.

The second event I wish to share about my early years at the university in pre-law is a good one in my opinion. I took this one class with about three hundred other students. Our professor would read to the class from a book written by an Ambassador Grew, who had been the ambassador to Japan. One day after the war had ended, he read during lecture two letters written from Grew to Roosevelt.

One letter was dated in April 1941 when Grew said the Japanese were going to attack the U.S. The next letter was dated in August 1941 when Grew said the site of attack would be Pearl Harbor. Obviously, we now know this is exactly what happened.

The third memory I have from my preparation for my law degree is historical. During my first two years at Washington University when I would arrive at school and get off the public transportation, I walked up steps to pass by a small cubical building which always had a man standing by it in surveillance. I learned later, after the war, this building covered some activity regarding research on the A-bomb. The Chancellor at the University at the time, Arthur Holly Compton, I recall, had some connection with this research. It amazes me to know that I was an inadvertent witness to such a integral part of our nation's history.

Something else happened during my tenure as a student at Washington University that, while at the time didn't seem very remarkable, has become somewhat pertinent to remember in light of recent events. During two of the summers I was in school, I worked. One summer I was at IBM and the other at General Motors, both in St. Louis. Coincidentally, I would later inherit some stock in General Motors from a great uncle who had worked at General Motors in St. Louis all his life. None of this is very memorable except that in 2011, all my stock shares were declared void when the government took over General Motors. Needless to say I was heart broken. In my opinion, this decision was contrary to all our dreams and history.

Well, I bring my university experience to a conclusion. All in all, my early life experiences were good. I had lived a comfortable, happy child hood, reared by parents who tried to help me do good by always looking to my Lord and Savior Jesus Christ for direction. This would be a path I would attempt to follow for the rest of my life.

Chapter Two

Crossing Paths In Missouri's Capitol

Do not be unequally yoked together with unbelievers,
for what fellowship has righteousness with lawlessness?"
2 Corinthians 6:14

After my graduation from law school, I recall two other notable experiences in my life relating to my legal direction.

One was my enrollment before the Supreme Court of the United States in 1954. A certain procedure is required for application and approval thereof and a motion by another attorney appearing before the court making a request for the enrollment.

My enrollment caused some considerable attention in newspapers all over the United States since I and my sister enrolled at the same time. As if two sisters simultaneously enrolling before the greatest judicial system in the world was not interesting enough, this occurred at a time when women were few and far between in the legal profession.

Author (right) and her sister on the steps of the
Supreme Court of the United States 1954

Author at Queen of England's Tea 1957

The second experience was attending bar meetings with the American Bar Association all over Europe in 1957. The first meeting was in London, England. The preparations by the Bar in England were quite ostentatious.

There was history in every step in England and I was very aware of this. We in the ABA enjoyed a visit to Parliament, an English court of law, and a trip on the Thames, and as a big final event, a tea at the palace garden with the queen and king of England in attendance.

After our time in London, we also enjoyed visiting Paris, France and finally Dusseldorf, Germany.

During this same period, I had taken a position in Jefferson City, Missouri working as an attorney with Legislative Research. I found the work to be very interesting, drafting bills, writing resolutions, and law articles.

Before I continue with my story, allow me to go back and give some background on Jim Noland, the man who would become my husband. During my history in St. Louis, my husband-to-be lived in Camden County, Missouri, a native of the county. I believe his mother encouraged him to go into the field of education. His mother and father both had a pure blooded American Indian ancestor, so that he is one-fourth American Indian. I am so proud that my children are one-eighth American Indian. He enlisted in the service in the Army Air Force. He re-enlisted and ended up in the Philippines at the latter part of the Second World War. Consequently, he was a member of the generation of service men that have now been entitled "The Greatest Generation."

When Jim Noland came home from service, he was entitled to what was called 52-20, or $20 a week for 52 weeks.

Jim did not take this. Instead, he worked for a neighbor who needed help in a sawmill and was paid $3.00 a day which amounted to $18.00 a week. He truly was part of the greatest generation.

Also, at this time he picked up and continued his education to become a teacher and educator. After he began to teach school he decided to run for political office. He elected to file for collector, and actually ran against the political boss in the county. In this first try he lost by only sixty votes. This might be discouraging to some, but now I know it was part of God's plan for our meeting.

In two years, after his first attempt for an elected office, my husband-to-be filed for the state legislature in Camden County, Missouri. This time he won by a big vote and in January of the next year went to Jefferson City.

There we were, both in Jefferson City. If he had won the original election he would never have come to Jefferson City. You have to learn to see the whole picture in your life. Sometimes things in life do not turn out as you planned, God has a much better plan.

Looking back, I realize Jim was the Christian for whom I had been praying. Likewise, I was the Christian my husband had been praying to come into his life. We were equally yoked.

Our wedding was very unusual. Other members of the House of Representatives in Missouri had been married in the House of Representatives. Naturally, everyone thought it obvious we should do the same. I wanted something more of a church atmosphere.

I thought the rotunda, with the beautiful staircase,

would provide a serene setting. However, this could only be accomplished with the permission of the governor, Governor Blair at the time. My betrothed, I was soon to learn, could command every situation and resolve problems with apparent ease. He went with a friend to Governor Blair's office to ask if this marriage setting were possible. The governor was very happy to comply with our request for the ceremony. We set the evening for March 26, 1958.

**Marriage Ceremony at Capitol Building
Jefferson City Missouri, March 26, 1958**

Janice Noland

The setting was, as I had imagined it would be, perfect; it was solemn and elegant. The fact that I could not see any of the stairs as I descended on my father's protective arm gave me all the security I needed. The arm of my Heavenly Father also gave me the assurance of strength, and the surety of my decision made this day truly special indeed.

The evening was over swiftly, and now I talk about it years later. We followed the biblical law and were equally yoked together. Why would either of us, my husband, a lawmaker, and myself, trained to be an instrument of the law, want to be associated with any lawlessness?

The laws of the world are constantly changing and their direction is influenced by good and evil, separately and deliberately. The laws of God are perfect and sure. GOD IS GOOD. Good should be the result of a Godly union and Godly nation.

Chapter Three

Teaching Our Children

All thy children shall be taught of the LORD,
and great shall be the peace of thy children.
Isaiah 54:14

After our marriage, and over a period of about ten years, God blessed our marriage with three daughters. Then the sharp realization came as to the depth of this responsibility.

Do we know as Christians how important it is to teach our children of the Lord? Over the years I have heard some parents say they did not want to indoctrinate their children, but let them make their own choices. I believe this is the paramount mistake any parent could ever make. In HIS WORD, the Lord clearly tells us we are to teach our children of Him.

Each of us is a free agent and if we find God and follow His Word and find the perfect directions for life, we have wisdom. As parents, we should help our children find their path to finding God, to ensure that they grow in wisdom.

Do we let our children cross the street in front of a car, put anything in their mouth where they might choose poison: certainly no good parent would allow such choices to be made.

> *"Foolishness is bound in the heart of a child."*
> *Proverbs 22:15.*

It is the parent's job to remove the foolishness. We must teach them wisdom in all areas of this life, and why then would we not teach them of eternal life the most basic wisdom of all?

My husband and I raised our three daughters, each born three years apart from one another. They received a standard for their life from my husband and me, just as each of our parents set a standard for my husband and me. Actually, I taught our daughters how to read out of the Bible before they went to school. This was a part of our home life since my husband set the standard of reading the Bible each night as a family. Why teach meaningless words, why not words for life? To read God's Word and live by the Word is good and produces good.

Consequently, even from a young age, my girls showed a touching and instinctive awareness of their relationship with their Creator. My youngest daughter, at the tender age of seven, wrote the sweetest letter we have ever received as parents. She thanked us for helping her with her homework and for "doing our best to help her love God." She had actual cognitive awareness and could put into words with total comprehension the concept of God and knowledge thereof.

My rearing of my children did not end in their young years. Even as young adults, I chose to continue advising them as to their spiritual walk. I carefully warned my children before they went to college; "Your Christian beliefs will be attacked." They knew it was coming, and my children were prepared. All three of my daughters, upon entering the college of their choice, were more prepared for the attacks than I had been. I did not expect the confrontation; they were made aware of this absolute prediction.

When my youngest daughter started college, her political science professor told her class of over three hundred students how he intended to teach evolution, and if any objected, "leave now." My daughter, the only one of three hundred, stood up and walked out.

Another daughter took a course in life and death. As she entered her college selection on the path to her career, on her final examination she told her professor of the plan of salvation and said, "...and you too will choose life or death."

Later, while in medical school, she confronted the Dean of the school when he addressed the class about abortion procedures. She respectfully asked how he could justify such procedures being performed by licensed physicians who had sworn to uphold the Hippocratic Oath. Her bold assessment was that such a blatant taking of innocent life was more in line with an oath of hypocrisy, to which she received no response. Several students approached her after the class to silently assent to her belief and position. She was shocked that so many agreed with her position and yet she alone stood in the gap to defend the lives of the innocent.

My oldest daughter was fortunately blessed with a college choice that posed no threat to her beliefs.

You can see the effect of teaching your children the truth of God.

Further generations become exponential, as each daughter shows our grandchildren the same truth they were taught by my husband and myself. My daughters had the discipline and understanding of how to stand firm and overcome the trials and tribulations of life. We can expect even more from the grandchildren. We can all see how our country is going more liberal as the left rises to influence our ways of thinking and living. No God in school, no Ten Commandments, we need to take our children out of schools where God cannot be taught. Against any and all odds we must teach our children of God. This is the law of God. This is the good fostered by following His Word.

Are you going to let any philosophy influence your children or are you going to make sure they know the truth? In Deuteronomy 6:4-9 it reads

> *4: Hear O Israel, the Lord our God is One Lord, :*
>
> *5:and thou shall love the Lord thy God with all thine heart and with all thy soul and with all thy might,*
>
> *6: and these words which I command thee this day shall be in thine heart,*
>
> *7: and thou shall teach them diligently unto thy children and shall talk of them when thou sittest in thine house, and when thy walkest by the way, and when thou liest down and when thou riseth up,*
>
> *8: and thou shall bind them for a sign upon thine hand, and they shall be as frontlets between thine eyes,*
>
> *9: and thou shall write them upon the posts of thine house and on thy gates.*

Chapter Four

Ministering Angels

"We are visited by angels unaware."
Hebrews 1:14

"For He shall give His angels charge over thee to keep thee in all thy ways."
Psalm 91:11

During the period that our children were attending college, which would have included 1978 to 1993, two miracles occurred. One happened when our youngest daughter was attending a university in Kansas. She had an art project late at night that she had to work on. As she left the classroom at two o'clock in the morning the walk towards her dormitory was a dimly lit and isolated journey. At the same time our second daughter awoke in Missouri from a strong conviction to pray for her family, as someone was in need. She continued in deep prayer for her family that lasted at least an hour. Meanwhile, at this exact time the youngest daughter saw a long grove of dark trees ahead and felt alarmed for her safety. At that moment she saw and described to me later, two large men (angels) suddenly appeared in front of her and entered the dark area with her, as she hurried safely to her dorm. Later she learned another girl from the campus was attacked in the same general areas where she felt unsafe. The suspect who was charged with a crime stated that the act had been at random but described seeing another girl that night flanked by two large men.

The second time an angel appeared to our family, happened when we were traveling in a caravan of three cars to Regent University Law School in Virginia Beach, Virginia. Our three daughters, my husband and I, and the items necessary for returning the girls to college that semester filled three cars. We stopped in Illinois about ten that evening. We went into a motel to spend the night and get some much needed rest. However, we were not happy with the room's upkeep and cleanliness and decided it was best to leave and drive on. When we went to the cars to continue our trip, my husband could not find the keys even when he returned to the room to search for them. We dejectedly went back out to the cars and sat on the curb wondering what we would do.

Out of nowhere appeared a fine looking gentleman who approached us, and he asked my husband what was wrong. As my husband explained to him about the locked car, he immediately started to give my husband directions on how to get into the car. He said, "Go to the front vent window on the drivers side, push the window in and reach through, you will be able to open the door. Now go over to the right side and slide open the door. Now reach on top of the clothes where you will find the keys you have misplaced."

When my husband followed these directions from the man, the keys were located and the van opened. As quickly as he appeared, he walked away into the night. Our middle daughter said to me, "We were just visited by an angel unaware." We were then able to drive to our destination in Virginia Beach. We had just experienced a miracle, the memory of which still blesses us today.

In the incidents related heretofore, the angels were present in form. Now I relate two true incidents where only the miracles were obvious.

One time my husband and I had attended a political meeting. My ten year old daughter at the time did not want us to go. I didn't ignore her fears, but felt we could be cautious. We parked in a parking garage by the door to go into the hotel. Later, when we came out of the meeting our car was close. However, before we got to the car, four individuals jumped out in front of us. I froze in terror, but instantly a glass wall went up in front of me and blocked the advance of the individuals only a foot from me. They ran into a stairway just ten feet away, Jim opened our car door, pushed me in, got in behind me and climbed over to the driver's seat. As the individuals reappeared, we backed out and drove away. Ministering angels put up the glass obstruction. Praise God for His goodness.

The other time I recall, Jim and I were driving home from a meeting. A vehicle passed us on a bridge, too fast for the slick conditions of the road. The vehicle went air born toward the ten foot high rock hill off the road. My husband said he prayed. We both saw the car turn in mid-air, back toward the road and set down in the grass. Ministering angels? Absolutely, we saw the vehicle directly reverse with our own eyes.

The next day, Jim happened to be at the same site, when a man and a young boy removed the vehicle. Jim stopped and told them what he had witnessed and how he had prayed.

The boy said, "Thank you," but the man was silent. How sad not to acknowledge the Lord's ministering control.

Finally, I need to relate an early visitation by angels my mother relayed to me early in my life. My mother had a sister who died before my mother was born. My mother's mother told her about the death of this young sister at age two. As she was dying, she said to her mother, "Oh look at the angels coming." How beautiful! How unrehearsed by a two year old.

The 91st Psalm is very depictive of the angels in this protective Psalm. I memorized it and said it over our daughters every day of their life as well as my own life and my husband's. Now we add grandchildren and friends in the need of prayer. This promotes God's Word in Jeremiah, there He says in Chapter 9:23-24

23. Thus saith the LORD; "Let not the wise man glory in his wisdom, neither let the mighty man glory in his might, let not the rich man glory in his riches:

24. But let him that glorieth glory in this, that he understands Me, that I am the LORD which exercise lovingkindness, judgment, and righteousness in the earth: for in these things I delight, sayeth the LORD."

The Bible describes angels in Hebrews 1:14 -

> *"Are they not all ministering spirits, sent forth to minister for those who shall be heirs of salvation?"*

Our testimony tells of the good they do.

Chapter Five

Politics

*"Most men will proclaim each one their own goodness,
but a faithful man who can find?"*
Proverbs 20:6

After my marriage and children, and while our children were being educated, my life became filled with the actual political arena for which my father had so diligently prepared me. As is the way I know with my Heavenly Father who was preparing me ahead of time, unbeknownst to me when I was a child at the knees of my earthly father.

My earthly father, a sincerely good citizen of the United States, taught me about the political parties, and being concerned and active in the system. I believe the main verb is being active with the desire to do good for our country being the main concern.

My father never ran for office, but the entire family was active in the political realm of the government. My father was president for one of the Republican wards of St. Louis. My family, including myself, carried and passed out the leaflets for the future candidates in the surrounding area. My mother worked as one of the election judges. When I became eligible to vote I worked as a watcher in the voting polls. I was to mark off what party each person was voting for as they requested the ballots to cast their vote.

My father was passionate that each party choose their own candidate.

I went to Republican meetings with my father. As I came away and read about it in the newspaper, I always commented to my father, "I was not at the same meeting the newspaper is describing." My father would comment, "The Post Dispatch appears communist, The Globe Democrat, Democrat and we Republicans have no newspaper."

Interestingly, my husband's family was also at work in the trenches at Macks Creek as my folks were at work in St. Louis City. My husband tells of one election his mother worked at the polls while it snowed. She could not walk home so she stayed at a neighbor's overnight. Can young people today, or anyone for that matter, envision no auto and no phone? But neighbors were good and people were seeking good. So it turned out well by helping one another. No government needed.

So much for my experience in politics before my marriage. After my marriage it was a new experience. Every candidate's wife knows at one time or another she will be called upon to speak for her husband. That time came for me and I could tell all my husband's education and experiences, but how could I express what kind of man I knew him to be.

In the Bible, I was reading in Proverbs at the time. The Lord directed me to go through the thirty one chapters verse by verse. I found the right one quickly,

"Most men will proclaim everyone his own goodness; but a faithful man who can find?" *Proverbs 20:6*

In my own home, where I was alone, I know I stood and shouted, "Halleluliah!" It was perfectly in point.

The people who spoke for office, then generally men, had good credentials and seemed likeable. I wanted to know about the heart of the man. With the verse that God gave to me I could tell everyone that I spoke to, my husband was a "faithful man." He is faithful to God. He reads the Bible to me every night. He is faithful to his country, he is a veteran. He is faithful to his family, we trust him anywhere, and he is faithful to his friends. He is always able to help solve their problems, able to find a good solution quickly, faithful to stand for good.

In selecting a candidate for any public office this is always a serious choice for me, choosing the right person. This goes beyond the facts, it goes to the heart of the one seeking office, it goes to being able to stand for good.

In over sixteen years my husband and I shared this purpose. He served eight years in the House of Representatives and eight years in the Senate of Missouri. When he ran for Senate, he ran against two incumbents where a new district had been formed. My husband was in a very busy campaign where he worked personally from early in the morning to late at night. By this time our children were in pre-school and grade school. We helped all we could, but my husband has always been diligent. He could be at work with important decisions to make, and never forget to bring home a miniscule item for his children.

Our family at the time of Jim's election to the senate.

During this time we were also building and adding to our home. We literally built separate additions, I believe about seven times over the years. Each time we adhered to the Bible directions;

"Unless the Lord builds the house, they labor
in vain who build it." Psalm 127:1.

My husband shared with me he had seen our house from the lake before he married me. Then after we purchased the land, he had a vision from the Lord each time about the addition. No other way could the original plan and the additions synchronize so outstandingly.

My husband won his election to the Senate after serving eight years in the House of Representatives. My mother and father were at our home when we called all the counties to get the results. They went home with the knowledge that my husband had won the election. The newspaper in St. Louis did not print the truth for several days. My mother called me believing I was in error, I was not. Well, my father had warned me years before about the press and the bias that would come from it. If we cannot know the truth, where do we find good or justice at the elections?

During my husband's term he told me of a time when the Senate session was closing as he took the floor and read the Bible for the last several hours in order to block some tax raises. This was a success and the taxes were never passed into law, he was able to uphold his convictions during this year. The Senate had a courtesy rule. No Senator could take the floor unless the one holding the floor released his control. Jim held the floor reading the Bible.

Justice can be claimed in many ways, but it gets less

and less available and fewer and fewer seek for good in the political system. Justice is lost in the too often search for personal favor.

Term limits went into effect after Roosevelt's four terms as president. The limit of two terms for the president was a good law. In my opinion, term limits presents the only formula to prevent entrenchment by unjust persons. Every office should have term limits. Congress, judges should be included.

In this connection, I wish to go forward several years, when my husband ran for Congress four times. Each time he won easily in the Republican primary.

Now in the general election, it was another story. In what was actually a Republican district, the vote reversed every time to the Democrat incumbent. This was a person we considered to be a good man, but we also confronted R.I.N.O.'s (Republicans in name only) in our own party every time in the four elections. They would say to me, "But the vote will go two-thirds to the incumbent in the general." I wondered how they could predict exactly. I knew they had not wanted my husband to win the primary. His popularity could not be overcome. But the general elections appeared controllable.

We had reason to suspect the voting equipment. Voting machines had come into play. Two counties in a district of 25 were hand counted, and these held to the primary vote. The machines went true to the prediction of the R.I.N.O.'s.

I want to quote from a book written by James M. Collier and Kenneth F. Collier in 1992, "Votescam: The Stealing of America" pg. 1:

"The authors assert, and back it up with daring reporting, that your vote and mine may now be a meaningless bit of energy directed by pre-programmed computers – which can be fixed to select certain pre-ordained candidates and leave no footprints or paper trail.

In short, computers are covertly stealing your vote."

This quote seems more obviously true with each ensuing election.

Chapter Six

Judge Janice

"All things work together for the good for those who know the Lord and are called according to His purpose." Romans 8:28

During the same period my husband was in the political office, suddenly the opportunity arose for me to run for judge in Camden County. Although it was my husband's recommendation and not my own idea, it seemed feasible. I recognized once again a man in my life, a man the Lord had provided for me, was suggesting the path I take. My father had done the same thing by suggesting I go into medical, law, education school etc. I had never considered being a judge, but after I graduated from law school my father had arranged through the mayor of St. Louis for my viewing the court room system there on a dias with one of the current judges. You had to be thirty years of age, and at the time I felt it would take forever to reach that age.

As time passes quickly, twenty years after this experience, I filed for judge in Camden County and was elected on the Republican ticket. I took office in January of 1970 and served for four years. I was not the usual judge. The Lord took precedence in my life, and I wanted to do good.

I decided to open court each time with prayer. Every new

day of a court session, I would invite a different minister, pastor or priest to come and give the opening prayer. The people stood for the prayer and then were seated. None of the lawyers appearing in court would enter into the court room until after the prayer was said and people were seated. Several lawyers asked me to stop opening with prayer in the court room, however, I held the line and continued to have the court opened with prayer. I could not see how we differed from our forefathers or our federal courts at this time.

Upon the walls of the court room during my term of office I also had two Bible verses framed and hung for all to see. The first was:

"The fruit of the spirit is love, joy, peace, gentleness, goodness, faith, meekness, temperance and long suffering; against such there is no law" Galatians 5:22.

The other sign read:

"Keep all the ordinances of men for that is the will of God, for with well doing you put to silence the ignorance of the foolish man." 1 Peter 2:15.

At the end of my four year term I refiled but did not ask one person to vote for me. The plea bargaining that I witnessed in court troubled me.

A plea bargain meant the prosecutor and the attorney for the defendant agreed to a charge of a lesser crime for a plea of guilty. This method might be merited in some cases where the case would be hard to prove and thus no consequence or restraint of the action alleged. However, releasing drunken drivers on the road seemed to present a potentially dangerous outcome for the public.

In fact I refused to go along with the bargaining. Because of that, the prosecutor encouraged defense attorneys to bypass my court by automatically appealing to a higher court. I encouraged mothers to come in and witness the procedures so they would understand how the law could be circumvented.

As the primary election came to pass it ended unbelievably in a tie. Three weeks later a run off election was held, and although it had been a Republican primary, in the run off everyone voted including the Democrats. To this day I doubt the legality of that election and the results that came from it. However, I knew the Democrats would not want the Republican candidate to win, nor did the lawyers.

Well, I have to say I was hurt over the loss. However, I later found that for me it was one of the best things that could have happened in my life. One Christian lady said to me, "There was nothing good or just in the election." I felt that was true, but not for me, because

> *"All things work together for good for those that love the Lord and are called according to His purpose."* Romans 8:28.

Within a month I was sitting in the courtroom on the dias alone, I felt the Spirit of God descend on me, and I received the baptism of the Holy Spirit so intensely I was never the same again. Instead of praying about every major decision in my life, I prayed all day long that every step I took was in God's will and that everything I did would bless Him.

All of us who know the Lord have a different walk, I would not be so presumptuous as to say you would have the same experience or even should have the same experience.

His blessings come from the same Spirit but in a different way. A beautiful, profound poem by Robert Louis Stephenson states:

> *"The best things in life are the nearest. The breath in your nostrils, the light in your eyes, flowers at your feet, the duties at hand, and the path of God just before you."*

However, in concluding this chapter, I want to add a principle I learned. "God can take the battle", but I believe that would include you doing good and doing all you can. I did not ask for one vote here. Can you believe I said, "If the public does not want a judge who does good and decrees justice, so be it?" And so it was! After this experience, my path encompassed directly, the search for the seeing of justice.

Chapter Seven

Life As A Lawyer

*"And thou knowest O man what is good, and what
is required of thee, but to do justly, to love equity,
and to walk humbly with thy God."* Micah 6:8

After politics, I again turned to the practice of law.

The potential influence of a lawyer or an attorney
is awesome as he or she attempts to represent clients or
groups. This power causes the public to look upon lawyers
with suspicion. People often perceive the corruption with
which this power is sometimes exercised. The Bible gives
us a glimpse of this perception in Luke 11:45-46 as Jesus
reproached the scribes and church leaders. One of the
lawyers addressed Christ saying to Him; *"Teacher, by saying
these things you reproach us also."* To which Christ answered;
*"Woe to you lawyers! For you have taken away the key to knowledge.
You did not **enter yourselves and those who were entering in
you hindered."***

Martin Luther addressed the same concept. When in
negotiations in Eislebn, Luther was trying to solve problems
by means of brotherly love, but lawyers, he said, "made it
difficult." *(Martin Luther the Great Reformer* pg 196 by Edwin
P. Booth)

When I began to use my knowledge of the law to address the affairs of individual clients, the Lord gave to me the importance of the verse by which this chapter is titled. I put it on my letterhead as my challenge. This also influenced my legal endeavors, my choice of cases, my selection of causes. If I felt someone to be wronged and justice had to be found, this was my cause.

Then as I worked privately in my legal profession I learned another truth. This involved my relationship with each client I was to represent. It was brought to my knowledge when my husband was reading to me from the Bible one evening from the book of Job. Job was speaking of God when he said;

1. *"For He is not a man as I am, that I may answer Him and we should go to court together.*

2. *Nor is there any mediator between us, who may lay his hand on us both.*

3. *Let Him take His rod away from me and do not let the dread of Him terrify me.*

4. *Then I would speak and not fear Him, but it is not so with me."*

Job was earnestly seeking an advocate to plead his case before God. I believe Jesus Christ became that advocate for me when I accepted Him as my Savior. Could I humbly perceive myself as an advocate for a client pleading, his or her case in court, just as Christ took my case for me?

This gives me a beautiful picture of the trial lawyer's role. I plead desperately sometimes, "Hear me judge, or jury. I am the advocate for the person I represent. I am telling you things you would not nor could not know. Hear me, this is not the same as the case before. This is not a person to be stereotyped and deprived of his uniqueness." This position of advocacy raised another requirement for me. I must believe in a client. I must believe his cause is righteous and he is telling me the truth. I cannot support a lie or an unjust cause."

By this time, I had arrived at certain beliefs about my role as a lawyer, and these beliefs became the dictates of my profession over the years to come.

The Lawyers Association of St. Louis
and
The Women Lawyers' Association of Greater St. Louis

Proclamation

*W*HEREAS HON. JANICE NOLAND ATTENDED LAW SCHOOL AND ENTERED THE LEGAL PROFESSION OVER FORTY-NINE YEARS AGO AT A TIME WHEN FEW WOMEN WERE PRACTICING LAW, AND IN SO DOING MADE THE WAY EASIER FOR FUTURE GENERATIONS OF FEMALE LAWYERS TO FOLLOW IN HER FOOTSTEPS AND ENTER THE PROFESSION OF LAW, AND

*W*HEREAS HON. JANICE NOLAND'S ACTIONS AND ACCOMPLISHMENTS DEMONSTRATE GREAT COURAGE, OPTIMISM, DILIGENCE, RESOURCEFULNESS AND PERSEVERANCE IN THE FACE OF GREAT OBSTACLES, AND ARE THUS WORTHY OF RECOGNITION DUE THEIR SOCIAL AND HISTORICAL SIGNIFIGANCE.

*N*OW, THEREFORE, ON THIS 24TH DAY OF OCTOBER 1996, WE THE PRESIDENTS OF THE LAWYERS ASSOCIATIONS OF ST. LOUIS AND THE WOMEN LAWYERS' ASSOCIATION OF GREATER ST. LOUIS EXPRESS CONGRATULATIONS AND APPRECIATION FOR HER CONTRIBUTIONS AND PARTICIPATION IN THE LEGAL PROFESSION.

MARK LEVISON, PRESIDENT,
ST. LOUIS LAWYERS ASSOCIATION

SALLY HELLER, PRESIDENT,
THE WOMEN LAWYERS' ASSOCIATION OF GREATER ST. LOUIS

Chapter Eight

Saving Our Lakefront Property

"Finally my brother, be strong in the Lord and the power of His might, put on the whole armor of God so that you may be able to stand against the wiles of the devil. For we wrestle not against flesh and blood, but against powers and principalities. Against rulers of darkness in this world, against spiritual wickedness in high places. So put on the whole armor of God so that you may be able to stand in the evil day and having done all, to stand; having your loins gird about with truth, having on the breastplate of righteousness, having your feet shod with the preparation of the gospel of peace, and especially taking the shield of faith wherewith you shall quench all the fiery darts of the wicked. The helmet of salvation and the sword of the Spirit which is the Word of God. Praying always for one another in the Spirit." Ephesians 6:10-18

This chapter relates to a case where my husband and I were the main parties and it turned out to be quite an experience. I personally believe every attorney going to court for another party needs to experience a case of his or her own. Where there is a personal involvement it really makes one understand the anxiety and stress of a client. It teaches an attorney patience and how to handle the retaliation and retribution when one's own rights have been taken away without any justification.

I remember vividly my husband and I went to a Gideon meeting the third Thursday of the month in November approximately 20 years ago. The next morning I got up and went to one of my windows to look at the view which I enjoyed every morning. There stood a high, multi-faceted boat dock almost in front of all our lake front. The neighbors had encroached surreptitiously, overnight on our lake front. We asked them to remove the dock, which was met with a refusal. When we contacted Union Electric, who at that time controlled the use of lakefront, they tried to help, but recognized the difficulty unless a lawsuit was filed.

My husband and I filed suit to force the removal of the dock from our property. I actually prepared the paperwork to be filed in the court. My husband was my star witness.

The trial did not come overnight for us. It took time and hard work, Union Electric company was on our side and confirmed our survey extended into the lake where we had owned the lake front rights for over forty years.

God showed me His presence all through this trial. My husband describes anything not affecting our lives in a personal way as being "at the barn." Thus, the lakefront was "at the barn."

Yet one day God showed me a blue heron with wings spread, walking my lakefront as though making a claim. Since that time I have noticed a blue heron perched on my boat dock periodically. I claim God's promise to me that I would be able to recover my land. Also, we began to put on Ephesians 6, the verses at the head of this chapter, every day as we went out into the world and face whatever we might encounter.

I came home one day and a survey marker, a red arrow,

was beside our mailbox; it was the arrow of the survey of the neighbors. They attempted to misrepresent our property line to gain additional land to the lake. I said, "Now Lord, you are showing me visually the fiery darts of the wicked." And indeed He was.

Two surveyors were hired, one by the defendant and one by us. They walked the ground together and through collusion agreed with one another on where the boundary lines should be set. My husband and I knew these boundary lines were wrong and we fired our surveyor. Instead, we had a neighbor who was able to confirm that our property line was indeed where we said it was. We then hired a third surveyor who had no personal interest in the case, who possessed copies of the original land plot. The defendant's surveyor bragged on the stand as to how many surveys he had performed in the past. My husband, sitting next to me said, "Ask him how many times he was wrong on those other surveys." It was such a good question, it ultimately made our case. The court ordered the dock be removed off our property line and defendant pay all our costs for court, including surveys and witnesses. We survived the ordeal and praised God.

Now, can you believe, ten years later, a new purchaser of the neighboring land brought in another monstrosity and parked it for nine months in front of our lakefront? We were in court again, praying for justice. Again the encroachment was removed and we recovered damages.

However, in concluding this chapter, I need to state a principle I learned strongly. I made a wrong decision, and didn't pray for the Lord's advice when the lady who sold our property to us offered to transfer ownership of this contested frontage also. No one could have encroached the way they have done over the years if I had taken this decision into prayer. With three children at my feet I said, "No, we don't want the extra land." I didn't think or pray for the right answer and now I know it was a blessing offered to us by God that I missed. I will never again say "yes" or "no" to any of life's questions without first asking my Savior for the right answer.

Chapter Nine

Perfect Justice In A Settlement

"And when a man's ways are right with God, he makes even his enemies to be at peace with him." Proverbs 16:7

After the dock fiasco, where the attempt was made to take over our lakefront, the land rights of my husband and I were violated again. I recall vividly I was having a luncheon at my lake house when I heard a loud boom and felt the shaking of my entire home. When I called the Osage Beach Police Department, I was told there was a blasting zone in my area to build a new condo addition on two lots to the right of me. When this blasting occurred, the concrete pool we had built in the lower part of our home was damaged from the force of the blast, not once, but twice. Both times they blasted, the pool walls developed seven individual destructive cracks, each about four feet long.

We had the indoor pool for years when about three hundred yards from our home, developers began building condos. In the course of the building, they blasted the bluff to make way for the foundation of the condo building. Within a week my husband discovered water was leaking out of our pool. This had never happened before. The only addition of water over the years was due to evaporation, and that was minimal. We knew something was wrong, and when we emptied the pool we found the damage on the sides of the pool from top to bottom. This made our pool now a danger to our home and on the verge of destroying all our belongings. We had to drain the pool that had been a part of our home for many years.

I obtained the names of the owners and contractors of the land where the construction was being done and wrote them a letter to advise them of the damages. I can say this did not bring about immediate relief. My husband had the cracks repaired in the pool as well as was correctable. The people who made the repairs were concerned that the patch work done would not hold and the pool would continue to be inferior. The contractors continued to blast and it was not too long until the pool began to leak again. We had to empty the pool again and get it repaired once more, in a different manner. We were in hopes the pool would hold the water in the condition it was initially.

We actually lost about a year of time where we were unable to use the pool. This was not a tolerable situation to the entire family. Although I did not like getting into the legal system there is a time we cannot overlook the situation and turn the other cheek. If the parties refuse to make right what they wronged, I filed suit and began the long trek towards justice: Answers, Interrogatories, Motions and Depositions for about two years.

The case was finally set for trial. One attorney on the other side was agreeable to mediation and so were we. As with many of my clients we did not want a monstrous amount and punitive damages for two times the damage, but we could reach what we considered a just amount. Over three days of trial and weeks of preparation for a result that no one could predict, was not advisable. The only result would probably be unjust to one side or the other and an appeals case could last forever.

The three attorneys for the other side and my husband and I chose mediation. From a list of three honorable, capable and retired judges one was chosen and we went to a mediation company in St.Louis.

This is a story in and of its self. My middle daughter who had helped me write some of the documents, decided to pray about an amount that would be just for all in the settlement. Then, I here in Missouri, and she in an eastern state in law school, each prayed separately. Believe it or not, when she and I shared our thoughts and insights, we had reached the same amount. So instead of a long trial in Camden County Missouri Circuit Court, my husband and I traveled to St. Louis to meet with the three opposing attorneys and the mediating judge. In the usual procedure for settlement, my husband and I were in one room, and the other three attorneys were in a separate room with their clients.

The mediating judge traveled between the two rooms discussing what had happened in the case, getting both sides of the story. It was his job to evaluate what would be just and fair. He had to decide on both the repair fees and the fact that it weakened the pool forever. Needless to say we were hours counseling with the judge trying to reach an agreement. The judge was patient in relaying demands and explaining differences. Finally, into the afternoon when the judge left our room I got up to walk and pray, "Lord, You take the battle now and give us justice." The offer came back and it was the amount my husband and I had agreed on, as well as the amount my daughter and I had received in prayer. We were satisfied with the settlement amount, but the best is yet to come. The other side was satisfied and we had reached an agreement. Mutual satisfaction of parties is unheard of in courts of law. Law schools, even Christian lawyers claim when you have a settlement or decision, no one is happy. Wrong! When God's justice was found, everyone was happy. I believe we saw perfect justice here.

Chapter Ten

The Glory of God In A Rural Courtroom

"and the court was full of the brightness of the Lord's glory," Ephesians 10:4

I also remember seeing real justice in the following account of a trial in a rural town.

I had a jury trial in Buffalo, Missouri one clear day. Buffalo is a nice, centrally located, rural town in the state of Missouri. Before I left home to travel to court, my husband and I prayed for our day. There were the usual anxious, stressful feelings as I drove to court that morning. I stopped for gas at a local station. The lady who owned it told me she was praying for the parties and myself in that day's hearing. This was typical of rural Missouri. Her words made me feel very grateful and my burden eased some as I got in the car again. Being a Christian I knew the power of prayer and many prayers. I continued my trip to the courthouse which is fifty miles from my home.

Once I arrived and sat down respectfully in the courtroom, the case was called. The parties and attorneys were all there, and the day began. Then all fell into place as it should and the momentum never ceased. It had begun, it will end, so concentration will take over. The morning progressed and the jury was selected. In my opinion this is the most important part of the case. One wrong person on the jury can reverse the entire decision. However, I recall no such error in this case. It was a rural area and all interrogation seemed to produce a jury with which my client and I were comfortable.

However, it was after we broke for lunch and I returned to the courtroom, a miracle occurred in this case that has made it live vividly in my memory forever. At 1 pm we reconvened the court. The parties, the attorneys, and the judge were all in their places. The defendant sat across from us with their attorneys. I cannot remember the attorney's name, but I do the judge. I sat at a table with my client. Suddenly, the feeling of love just enveloped me as I sat there. As I thought of my husband and children, the feeling of love was completely overpowering. Then I looked across the table at my opponents, and I felt compassion, a quiet peace and gentleness. Not the usual competitiveness that is present in the courtroom.

Have you ever been aware you are witnessing the "glory of the Lord?" Do you believe you know what the "glory of the Lord" looks like? I had one client who shared with me that she had been in the presence of the Lord and witnessed His Glory. She had read the Bible through fifty times. This was an amazing testimony, as it brought forth the idea that I could really enter into the presence of the Lord. Surely others have sought this splendor. It came upon me completely unexpected and unannounced. Can you believe I was in a court room, an honest to goodness court of law with a judge and jury.

Then it was like the entire front of the courtroom became bathed in this golden aura like a spotlight in a theater. I knew the Glory of God was in that courtroom. From that moment forward the trial became easy, every question put on my mind flowed freely. I felt the Spirit of the Lord commanding the process. Every answer to my questioning was perfect for our case. And finally, when the opposing witness answered "yes" to the question, "Are you a drinking buddy of the person for whom you are testifying" it was won.

The jury came back with a decision for my client, and we were home free. The judge said to me, "You enjoyed that?" I did not share with him what I had experienced that day. I have since discovered some words in Ezekiel absolutely descriptive of my experience. In chapter 8, verse 1, Ezekiel describes *"that the hand of the Lord God fell there upon me and the appearance of brightness as the color of amber."* I found this verse some time after my experience and it fits so perfectly the colors I saw in the courtroom that day. Praise the Lord; His Spirit never changes. I saw justice prevail in the presence of God's Glory. I believe I was the only one in the courtroom who saw the glory that day. I need to share it now.

Chapter Eleven

A Fly On The Wall

"For God hath chosen the foolish things of the world to confound the wise and; God hath chosen the weak things of the world to confound the things which are mighty." 1 Corinthians 1:27

As I recall past accounts and experiences I had within the courtrooms of Missouri, I can't help but recount another trial I considered miraculous. It took place in the rural community of Warsaw, Missouri in Benton County.

The courthouse was on the square right downtown. The courtroom was on the second floor and the benches and dais contained dark brown wood, very regal looking. It was a summer day, beautiful and tranquil. As my husband and I drove to Warsaw, we were soaking in the raw beauty surrounding us. I always loved it when he was available to drive me as we were such a team. He always had such tremendous insight.

I was nervous, as I always was when I faced a jury trial. Strangely enough, however, as soon as the trial started, the nervousness stopped and my mind was targeted on finding and seeing justice.

The suit involved the charge of carrying a concealed

weapon. The prosecutor had offered my client, in exchange for a plea of guilty, a suspended imposition of sentence and two years probation. What this basically meant was if this period of time lapsed and my client encountered no other criminal incidents, then the charge would disappear and he would have no criminal record. My client did not want an agreement; he wanted a trial.

The incident that had been the basis for the criminal charges had arisen at my client's farm. A man had come onto his property to collect a bill. My client, in response, had run the man off his property, and the intruder claimed my client had wielded a gun.

I had learned to make a habit of asking the Lord for His wisdom in selecting jurors. Even one juror can spoil the entire panel. In a criminal matter, all jurors must unanimously agree in order for a conviction. This is unlike civil matters where only three-fourths of a twelve person jury decides an issue.

As I stated above, this was a rural area. With that came the likelihood there would be a more conservative pool of jurors from which to choose a jury. Also, many of the prospective jurors in such an area tend to be of a more advanced age. This lends itself to a pool of prospective jurors with more expansive life experiences. The hope then, at minimum, becomes one of the potential for greater wisdom.

It took most of the morning to empanel the jury. I did it carefully, questioning each juror individually so I could get to know them. I can't recall any problem making the selections. This was Benton County; a place where I felt infinitely more comfortable compared to other jurisdictions.

The prosecutor presented his case first. He had the gun

which he alleged was concealed by my client at the time of the incident. The prosecutor's portion of the case was completed before lunch.

I recall I had started with my first witness when we broke for lunch. My husband and I walked to a local restaurant. Even my selection of food was important. No large, heavy lunch. Cottage cheese, iced tea and protein were my selections.

My husband Jim instructed me to something as seemingly insignificant as to my position in the courtroom. He told me he thought it would be helpful if I were to move to the left of the jury. This would enable me to more effectively gain the full attention of the jury as they would be forced to look in my direction.

"Don't stand directly in front of the jurors," he adroitly explained. Make them want to look to you, so they will pay attention to what it is you are saying.

While this was rational and insightful advice, in the din of ideas rushing through my mind, it soon dissipated. Consequently, upon reentering the courtroom, I proceeded to present my case from my original location. I had completely forgotten my husband's sage advice, being intent only on my questioning.

Almost unbelievably, in a closed courtroom, fully air-conditioned, out of nowhere, a huge fly flew right into my face. Try as I might, I could not wave it away. I was forced to move away from the spot this pesky fly was so determined to dominate. It was then that I remembered my husband's directions. I moved to the very position my husband had directed. The amazing thing was that once I did, the fly was nowhere to be seen.

After I moved to the better position in front of the jury the case developed much more expediently. I had to prove through my only witness, my client himself, that he had no concealed weapon. Further, even if he had wielded a weapon, the fact remained that he had been on his own property, fully vested with the right to protect himself.

In the examination of my client, he placed the gun in the pocket of his clothing that he had been wearing on the day of the charge, and he was able to show the gun could not be concealed in his pocket. Rather, it would have been very apparent.

"Put the gun in the pocket as you did on the day the prosecutor claims you had a concealed weapon." When my client followed my instructions the firearm was almost fully exposed.

"Did you tell the intruder to leave your property?"

"Yes."

"Was your gun as you exhibited evident as it appears today?"

"Yes."

Twelve jurors unanimously came in finding the defendant "not guilty." My client was fully exonerated of any wrong doing. Haleluliah! What a wonderful feeling for both my client and myself!

After the trial when I went over to thank the jurors, one man who identified himself as the foreman, said, "You just struck a blow today for the right to keep and bear arms." This juror further identified himself as a former member of the military. I hear his words ringing in my memory today.

"You just struck a blow today for the right to keep and bear arms!" What a wonderful constitutional victory from such a seemingly insignificant case!

With all the stress of the trial with a jury, to witness such a miracle anywhere, and especially in a court of law, was tremendous and awesome.

Chapter Twelve

Quick Justice In the Court of Appeals

"Doth our law judge any man before it hear him and know what he doth?" St. John 7:51

When you take this quote from the Bible, it is obvious that such a denial of due process, which in layman's terms means notice and an opportunity to be heard, should never happen in the courts of law in the United States. I quote this verse from the Bible because we used it in a case before the Court of Appeals, in the State of Missouri. This was a case where we had to go to the higher courts because the lower court did exactly what the verse says should never happen.

Our firm conducted this case from beginning to end. It involved a relatively simple matter and not a huge sum of money. However, a judgment was entered by an associate court judge without there ever being a hearing.

The trial was located right across the street from my office. Actually, a simple telephone call would have prevented this extreme and obvious miscarriage of justice. Through some oversight of the court, our office had never received notice of the setting and, accordingly, neither I, nor my client, was present for the hearing.

This was the situation. We had not received notice from the clerks' office of the date and time of the hearing. No attorney would deliberately ignore the courts message. My client and I were both willing to sign an affidavit we had no knowledge of the hearing. (Note: once counsel is entered into a case, all notices go directly to counsel rather than directly to the party.) The only knowledge my office had of the hearing came when we received a copy of the judgment written by the judge and sent to my firm by mail.

Of course, I was upset and immediately, in accordance with the civil procedure, filed a motion to set the judgment aside and set the case for an actual real trial on a date of which we had knowledge. In my opinion, to question our failure to appear without reason was a position untenable, as no one would be expected to miss a hearing deliberately. A simple hearing seeking justice would have appeared advisable under the circumstances, unless there was a deliberate intent to uphold a miscarriage of justice.

To make matters worse, the judge rendering the judgment refused to simply set it aside and reschedule a hearing. Of course, we filed an appeal. This was not a criminal matter and no wrong could have resulted by setting a hearing. We had no option but to file in the court of appeals to remand the case for trial.

This is when the Lord provided a sequence of a series of miracles which took place. I was driving from my office in Camdenton to my home fourteen miles away. Traffic was horrible due to new construction on the roads. I had to slow the car to a maximum speed of five miles per hour. I rolled the windows down and looked for a tape to play in the stereo. My mother had recently passed away and the tapes I had given her to listen to, the New Testament, were in my car. I started to play the New Testament tape.

It was then that I heard the clarion voice of the Lord through His written word in John 7:51 -

> *"Doth our law judge any man before it hear him and know what he doth?"*

Oh my goodness; that was exactly what had happened to us in the case which we had just filed in the court of appeals! My mind exploded. I decided right then that I would use that Bible quote in our brief.

My middle daughter had just graduated from Regent University Law School in Virginia Beach. She was well versed in Blackstone's commentaries. For the reader's information, the commentaries were a thorough exposition on the body of law that came from England to our country. It was the unwritten and universal law of God as written on the hearts of man. It was the understanding that any law that did not align with the will of our Maker as revealed by Him in His holy scripture, was not valid law.

My daughter recommended a statement from Blackstone. I went to Jefferson City to the Supreme Court Library to find the quotation we wanted in our brief. Blackstone's commentaries were in the basement of the Supreme Court building in the archives, symbolic of how they had been forgotten by our society and hidden away from view.

I am going to quote for you here how my daughter used the Bible and Blackstone's Commentaries in her brief.

Blackstone defined the law of the land as follows:

"The law of the land is obviously that law applicable to those subjects as citizens of the land....and if our reason were always.... clear and perfect....we should need no other guide but this. But every man now finds the contrary in his own experience, that his reason is corrupt, and his understanding full of ignorance and error. This has given manifold occasion for the benign inter- position of the divine. Providence which, in compassion to the frailty, the imperfection, and the blindness of human reason, hath been pleased, at sundry times and in divers manners, to discover and enforce its laws by an immediate and direct revelation." (Blackstone's Commentaries pp.29- 31)

Again she said, *"So then, the question comes, what if anything does this superior authority have to say about a case such as the one at bar? The Holy Scripture says, "Doth our law judge any man before it hear him and know what he doth?" St. John 7:51. Therefore, if this judgment is upheld without affording the defendant his right to be heard, then it will be upheld in direct contravention to the United States Constitution, the Missouri Constitution, the common law of the land, and the Superior Authority of the will of the Maker. We humbly request that the case be remanded and defendant be allowed his day in court."*

Thus, she quoted the Bible and Blackstone's Commentaries along with current law as authority for reversal of the judgment in our appeals case.

I now recall the next miracle that happened. As we appeared in the Court of Appeals in Springfield, Missouri for an oral argument, the other attorney declared their theory of their case. I never said a word.

One of the three judges stood up and said, in essence, "I have been on the bench for twenty years and have never given a decision before I leave the court room." Then he said, "This case should be remanded and the judgment set aside for hearing."

When I started to speak, I caught the almost imperceptible "no" shake of the judge's head as if to direct me that I need not say a word in my defense. I sat down, what was there to say after that? I learned something that day. "Less truly is more," especially when justice prevails and is seen so obviously.

Chapter Thirteen

Further Pursuit of Justice

"Justice, Justice thou shall pursue." Deuteronomy 16:20

In my pursuit of justice over my years in practice, besides the awesome cases I have described, smaller favors have occurred wherein I felt I saw justice, and these experiences I describe as follows:

Linn, Missouri

In one of my trials I traveled to Linn, Missouri on a custody and child support matter. I remember pulling into town and the courthouse was directly attached to the highway which veered through the town. After parking across the street from the courthouse I crossed the highway and entered the courthouse. I went to the second floor, where the courtroom was located. The view from the windows of the courtroom was incredible. It was like one was looking at a lovely pastoral painting. Quiet, quaint, picturesque, rolling farm hills spanned the horizon; not at all what I had witnessed from other courtrooms.

When the judge came in he told us he had been praying for his wife who was ill. How unusual to find a judge not afraid to speak of God. The case was resolved before the day was over in a manner I considered just, fair and equitable for all. The problem was gone. It always amazes me when a judge seeks understanding, how he is able to then exhibit the wisdom of Solomon. Such wisdom is seen all too rarely, but I did witness it that day in that beautiful courtroom.

As is the custom, I went into one room with my client. The other attorney went into a separate room with his client. Then the two attorneys met in a third room to convey the wishes of their respective clients. We are usually way apart in trying to reach an agreement; not only acceptable to each client, but hopefully somewhat fair to each client. Experienced attorneys know about where this border lies for each client. I personally would never agree to something I could not have lived with myself. If no agreement could be reached, then the judge would proceed to try the case.

On this particular day we could not reach an agreement, so we went to the courtroom and appeared before the judge. No long and arduous trial was required. Usually such an action results in more frustration and further bad feelings between the parties, which interferes with the family involved. On this day, however, the judge questioned the parties for summation, the probing wisdom of the judge who conducted the hearing, with his kindness and compassion to all involved, was equally just and equitable to both parties. We all understood his wisdom and rationale. Through a godly judge, justice comes swiftly.

Federal Court, Jefferson City, Missouri

I remember an amazing case held in the Federal Court in Missouri. It involved a criminal charge, serious, but not life or death. The federal prosecutor considered my client a criminal, the probation officer treated my client like a number, thus enabling the system to decide on a "blanket" degree of punishment. I felt compelled to tell the judge, prior to the court hearing, that I was my client's advocate and would be pleading on his behalf just as Christ had pled for me.

Knowing what I was going to say, during the case in the courtroom the judge asked me to repeat exactly what I had told him in the back room; that I was indeed my client's advocate. Amazingly, after that all information concerning the case was thoroughly examined. All parties involved, myself, opposing counsel and the judge, were then able to come to a resolution that would ultimately prove just for my client.

Holden, Missouri

A case in Holden, Missouri brought forth yet another miraculous happening in my legal career. This location was outside my general region of practice. Again it was a quiet area with a peaceful tranquility surrounding it. I had traveled to the area the night before to be there because of the distance I had to drive, for a dissolution hearing, otherwise known as a divorce. I arrived at seven in the evening and had several hours to study for the trial preparations. I also had taken a book called *"Favor"* which centered on Psalm 3 where it says, ***"the righteous are encompassed with favor as with a shield."*** The book was not too long to read but a wonderful message. Many times we forget to accept our blessings. I read and claimed *"Favor."*

The next day I and attorney for the other client entered the judge's chambers. This was an extremely common practice for parties counsels to be able to review a case, see where it stands and to see if it can be settled. The judge in this instance indicated how he found the facts and how he would see the settlement. This conclusion was not satisfactory to the opposing client. She released her attorney so she could get another attorney and have the case delayed. I only share this to show the effectiveness of prayer for favor made by me prior to our appearance

Paris, Missouri

Another travel I recall of interest was a trip to Paris, Missouri, not to be confused with Paris, France. When I arrived at the courthouse, the elevator was not working so the judge very kindly moved his session of court to the first floor for everyone's convenience. The other attorney and I had a friendly but professionally-based relationship. Given the kindly judge and the amicable attorneys it was settled in the best interest of the minor child of the marriage.

This case had a wonderful ending. Later I received a letter from my client thanking me for believing in his child and settling with the other attorney in her best interests, so she was now fulfilling her academic dreams.

In all cases where I saw justice, the justice I pursued, the formula was the same, a judge and two attorneys who were aware of and who appeared to be exercising the following directive:

> *"Thou knowest, O man, what is good and what is required of thee; to do justly, to love equity, and to walk humbly with thy God."* Micah 6:8.

Particularly in personal matters involving marriage and children, unless the above justice can be achieved, I believe the only relief for a Christian is in following the words of the

Bible found in 1 Corinthians 6: 1-6 that advises to refrain from going to court before the unjust:

1. *Dare any of you, having a matter against another, go to law before the unjust and not before the saints?*

2. *Do ye not know that the saints shall judge the world? And if the world shall be judged by you, are ye unworthy to judge the smallest matters?*

3. *Know ye not that we shall judge angels? How much more things that pertain to this life?*

4. *If then ye have judgments of things pertaining to this life, set them to judge who are least esteemed in the church.*

5. *I speak to your shame. Is it so, that there is not a wise man among you? Not one that shall be able to judge between his brethren.*

6. *But brother goeth to law with brother, and that before the unbelievers.*

Chapter Fourteen

Describing Justice

*"Many seek an audience with a ruler, but it is
from the Lord that man gets justice."*
Proverbs 29:26 – NIV

In years of seeing the legal practice in court it is my conclusion that justice comes occasionally, not frequently.

Justice is always depicted as a woman with her eyes covered, giving the impression that justice can only come without prejudice, as long as there is no former knowledge and cannot be seen. I may agree with this as far as a secular, earthly concept of the word justice. However, I have found a different answer in my practice.

"Many seek an audience with a ruler, but it is from the Lord that man gets justice." *Proverbs 29:26 – NIV.*

God is not blind, He is not prejudiced, He is perfect justice. This will not totally agree with man and his perception of justice, but there will be no fault or flaw. I learned this during my practice. I know I had some really awesome cases. I have shared a few with you in this book.

When my youngest daughter and I had been to court

together all day after she became an attorney, sitting there beside her she said to me, "Mother, when you got justice in the courtroom it was a fluke." That statement threw me back into my chair. That could not be true, or could it? The answer came to me in about a week, as I was eating lunch at my desk in my office. The Bible lay open before me, my eyes fell on the words *"Many seek an audience with a ruler, but it is from the Lord that man gets justice."* Of course that was the answer, and yes, the cases I remembered were miraculous as they played out before me. Reflecting on the outcome of the cases as I recounted them in my mind, my memory was clear on the Godly influence that was there with me. Each time I felt His presence. It always, to the best of my knowledge, would only happen if all members of the judicial process were Christians.

The pool case settled to all sides being satisfied. The attempted stealing of our lakefront property, when the Lord walked with me even to show me the arrows of the devil, and the power of God with the blue heron walking the waterfront to claim it. All these accounts were and are miraculous, some not as dramatic as others, but still showing the hand of the Lord God.

Sometimes, I saw players changed to receive and finally see justice, but when the players are not in accord with the precepts of Christ to do good and see justice, justice appears to be imperceptible.

Chapter Fifteen

Doing Good Not Evil

The Bible tells us -

"the fear of the Lord is the beginning of wisdom." Psalm 111:10.

"The wisdom of the Lord is to hate evil, and the evil
way, and the froward mouth." Proverbs 8:13

I did not know the word froward. I had never seen it except in this verse. I looked it up in the dictionary and the definition is: "perverse." Everything contrary to God's law is the meaning as I read it. That continues the thought of evil. The devil is evil; God is good. Each concept contains it's own meaning. I have come to answer the question, "How are you?" by saying, "Good not evil." This always creates a smile or a stir of reaction which is what I mean to incite.

The Bible said to me and I put on my stationary:

"And thou knowest O man what is good, and what is
required of thee, but to do justly, to love equity, and to
walk humbly with thy God." Micah 6:8

Additionally, the knowledge of good has come to me in my life from various other sources, for example:

1. The Declaration of Independence for my wonderful country said in paragraph 2:

"We hold these truths to be self-evident, that all men are created equal, that they are endowed by their Creator with certain unalienable Rights, that among these are Life, Liberty and the pursuit of Happiness."

2. Ellen White wrote "The Great Controversy." It was given to me by the Seventh Day Adventist when I was elected judge. The message in her book is "good versus evil; God versus the devil; from day one to the present this has been the battle. The devil has become rampant in these latter days, but the devil has been overcome. The efforts of evil to overcome good is obvious in America today.

3. When my husband was a legislator in Missouri, I was at home with three small children. During this time I read the Christian Science Monitor. In it, Mary Baker Eddy, a Christian Scientist, emphasized the knowledge of the 91st Psalm. I was impressed with this protection Psalm. I memorized it, and literally prayed it over my children as they grew, and as they went forward on their own as young adults. It proved to be a wonderful source of comfort for me.

4. My husband was Grand Master of the Missouri Masonic Order for one year, governing 100,000 men. He shares with me the fraternity, not a religion, promotes brotherly love, relief and truth. I am a member of Eastern Star, which is the women's Auxillary Organization of the Masons. The function of this organization is to study and portray five exemplary women of the Bible. We study Adah, the daughter; Ruth, the widow; Esther, the wife; Electa, the mother; and Martha, the sister. I always prefer to be Esther. I admire/am astounded by the way she was able to achieve life

and justice for her people who were captives in the Persian Empire. This story of this one woman's pursuit of good over evil has had international and timeless impact. Just recently Netanyahu, of Israel, appeared on television when he was here in America. He said, "I must mention a young woman," and to my delight, he recalled the story of "Esther."

Masonic Meeting

5. Of course, I have related my Lutheran background by my parents for seventeen years before I went to college. I memorized the Bible. I recall,

"Train up a child in the way he should go and when he is old he will not depart from it." *Proverbs 22:6.*

I believe embedding the Lord's statutes deep into the life of our children is essential to winning the fight between good and evil.

6. Later in life I was exposed to <u>"Handel's Messiah"</u> as a performer in the local chorus with a group of people from the area. When we performed that Christmas and concluded with the <u>"Halleluiah Chorus"</u> it suddenly came to me strong and clearly. "Oh how the man who wrote this knew the Lord." About two weeks later, I read in the Lutheran Witness how Handel, a grandson of a Lutheran pastor wrote this masterpiece in three weeks in his attic. When he came down to a servant in the house, Handel said, "I perceived I was at the throne of the great God Himself." I said, "I knew it, I knew it! The Spirit of God is always the same." I was able to recognize this truth as I performed in the program that Christmas

7. I watch Brigham Young University television. They advertise they are able to see the "good in the world." Certainly their chorus is magnificent in displaying this awesome good. When their choir performs the <u>"Halleluiah Chorus,"</u> it is a foretaste of heaven. Also, I have to mention a dissertation I viewed of the description of the Lord in Revelation 19 where the Lord is described as *"having a sword come out of His mouth."* This blessed me because every day for many years my family prays on the whole armor found in Ephesians 6 which describes the sword of

the spirit as "the Word of God." I found the sword described several times in Revelation and to me this is a profound confirmation of the entire Bible which describes,

> *"In the beginning was the Word, and the Word was with God and the Word was God, and the Word became flesh and walked among us."* John 1:1-4.

8. The Catholic church has been relentlessly pursuing good by pursuing the Will of our Maker in the area of education. Through their willingness to take on the responsibility of holding themselves accountable for the education of their children, their children are excelling academically. In an era when most have simply thrown away their parental responsibility to educate, such a conviction is rare and should be applauded.

9. I need to mention the Gideon's and my own courtroom; when both of us testified to a man who appeared before me in court and the Gideon's witnessed to him in jail while awaiting trial in my courtroom. I saw the fruit of our persistent labors when years later the young man who had stood before me in court returned to Camden County to ask me as an attorney to change his name to a Biblical name, thus being able to reflect his new way of life that had begun in a courtroom years earlier.

10. Something that happened just recently blessed me. I watched the wedding of Prince William to Kate Middleton on television in the last year. In the ceremony I heard the Arch Bishop say, "Hate evil and hold fast to that which is good." I am aware that God's word is found in all reaches of the universe. If you will recall I attended the Queens tea years ago and I find this conviction of God's word years later in a grandson's wedding a huge blessing.

There are others that promote good. I may not know all of them, and I could not relate all of them here, but if they preach salvation by Christ the Lord, they are speaking the truth and are brothers and sisters in Christ.

I want to add here a few lines from a poem brought to my attention recently in a political meeting of the Missouri Republican Assembly in Springfield. I read:

> *"Once to every man and nation comes the moment to decide*
> *In the strife of Truth with Falsehood, for the good or evil side."*

I did not know who had written this poem, but my daughter found it was written two centuries ago and entitled <u>"The Present Crisis"</u> by James Russell Lowell

I again praised the Lord for having me locate this source right at a time when I had come to a similar conclusion.

Have you made your choice for the good or evil side?

Chapter Sixteen

A Standard for the Followers of Jesus Christ

"and where the Spirit of the Lord is there is liberty."
2 Corinthians 3:17

Dear reader, I am bringing this testimony to a close, but the most important question needs to be asked of you: Do you know the Lord Jesus Christ as your Savior?

<u>John 1:1</u> *"In the beginning was the Word, and the Word was with God, and the Word was God.....and the Word became flesh and walked among us."*

<u>Jeremiah 9:23</u> *"Let not the wise man glory in his wisdom, let not the strong man glory in his strength, let not the rich man glory in his riches, but let he who would glory, glory in this; that he knows and understands Me and I am the Lord who exercises loving kindness, judgment and righteousness in the earth."*

<u>2 Peter 4:6</u> *"And God who commanded the light to shine out of darkness has shined in our hearts to give the light of the knowledge of the glory of God in the face of Jesus Christ."*

<u>Jude 1:24</u> *"unto Him who is able to keep us from falling,*

and is able to present us faultless before the presence of His glory, to the only wise God our Savior, be honor and glory and dominion of power now and forever. Amen."

I have shared and reshared with you God's words which speak to me so strongly now I share with you the words He gave to me to explain my faith.

AND WHERE THE SPIRIT OF THE LORD IS, THERE IS LIBERTY:

II Corinthians 3:17

"I AM THAT I AM"
SAITH OUR LORD GOD ALMIGHTY
AND IN QUIET HUMILITY SPEAKS
HIS DIVINITY,
HIS MAGNIFICANCE,
HIS WISDOM,
HIS LOVE,
PERFECTION: ULTIMATE: ABSOLUTE,
"I AM THAT I AM"

AND WHO AM I?
WHAT CAN I SAY OF ME?
AT BEST, I AM THE LEAST,
LIMITED IN ABILITY,
BOUND BY THIS BODY,
BOUND BY MY MIND,
NARROW,
IMPERFECT, SEARCHING, LACKING
THAT IS WHO I AM.

BUT WHO CAN I BE?
WITH THE BAPTISM OF THE HOLY SPIRIT
AS THE LORD ABIDES IN ME,
I SEE THE WORLD WITH HIS EYES
I SEE HIS CHILDREN WITH HIS LOVE,
I PARTAKE OF HIS KNOWLEDGE,
HIS UNDERSTANDING,
HIS POWER,
NOW I KNOW NO BOUNDS; I AM SET FREE
HE LIVES IN ME.
Copyright 1976 by Janice P. Noland

STANDARD

I want to propose a standard for all followers of Jesus Christ:

1. Find God through the Lord Jesus Christ

2. Hate evil – *Psalm 97:10*

3. Hold fast to what is good – *1 Thessalonians 5:21*

4. See justice

My prayer for you is:

And finally my brothers (and sisters) be strong in the Lord, and in the power of His might.

Put on the whole armour of God, that ye may be able to stand against the wiles of the devil.

For we wrestle not against flesh and blood, but against principalities, against powers, against the rulers of the darkness of this world, against spiritual wickedness in high places.

Wherefore take unto you the whole armour of God, that ye may be able to withstand in the evil day, and having done all, to stand.

Stand therefore, having your loins girt about with truth, and having on the breastplate of righteousness;

And your feet shod with the preparation of the gospel of peace;

Above all, taking the shield of faith, wherewith ye shall be able to quench all the fiery darts of the wicked.

And take the helmet of salvation, and the sword of the Spirit which is the Word of God:

Praying always with all prayer and supplication in he Spirit, and watching thereunto with all perseverance and supplication for all the saints; Ephesians 6:10-18

AMEN!

Addendum

On March 26, 2008 we celebrated our 50th wedding anniversary at the rotunda of the Missouri Capitol Building.

As this date was approaching, I realized I would like my celebration to be at the same place as our wedding.

As God would allow, some months prior to the date, I was at a meeting with the then governor of Missouri, Matt Blunt. I told him as I met him in line, "I have a request. May I say it now or later?" He graciously said, "Now." I told him I had been married in the rotunda, and I would like to return there for celebration of my 50th Wedding Anniversary. He said, "I will have to verify with the building commission." About a week later I received a call from the commissioner. He said, and I believe I quote exactly, "We want to make it happen." What a wonderful statement. My daughters saw that it happened. The following pages are pictures thereof.

To Celebrate 50th Wedding Anniversary
In honor of the 50th Wedding Anniversary of James and Janice Noland friends and relatives are cordially invited to join them as they renew their wedding vows Wednesday evening, the 26th of March at half after seven o'clock in the Rotunda of the State Capitol Building, Jefferson City, Missouri. Reception immediately after the ceremony. The James and Janice were married March 26, 1958.

50th Anniversary Announcement

50th Anniversary with children and grandchildren

Jim and Janice on the steps of the Capitol Rotunda

Author Bio

Janice P. Noland is a fourth generation American, whose grandparents recall immigrating to America from Prussia. She is a graduate of Washington University School of Law and, prior to retirement, practiced law in excess of 60 years. During that time she served as a Bill Drafter in Legislative Research for the Missouri Senate and House of Representatives. She drafted a publication for West Publishing detailing the methodology of statutory construction. She served as the first City Attorney for the City of Osage Beach, Missouri and as Probate and Magistrate Judge for the County of Camdenton, Missouri. Her varied legal experiences spanning the course of well over half a century shed luminous insight into the pursuit of justice.